The DC Eagle Cam Project

MR. PRESIDENT
and THE FIRST LADY

Teena Ruark Gorrow & Craig A. Koppie

In Cooperation with the **American Eagle Foundation**

Schiffer Publishing Ltd

4880 Lower Valley Road • Atglen, PA 19310

Photo credits: Front cover: Courtesy of the American Eagle Foundation. Back cover: Courtesy of the American Eagle Foundation in cooperation with the US National Arboretum. Front Flap: © Craig A. Koppie.

All screen-captured photos derived from the DC Eagle Cam live-streaming cameras are © 2015–16 American Eagle Foundation (AEF) and provided courtesy of the AEF in cooperation with the US National Arboretum (USNA) unless otherwise noted. Other photographs are © Teena Ruark Gorrow or © Craig A. Koppie, or provided courtesy of the AEF; Sue Greeley, USNA; Jeff Jacobsen; Laura Jacobsen; Craig A. Koppie, US Fish & Wildlife Service (USFWS); John D. Prickett; Dan Rauch, Department of Energy & Environment (DOEE); Jeff Stevens, Alfred State SUNY College of Technology, New York; or Richard Suter Photography as noted.

Cover and Interior designed by Matthew Goodman
Type set in Mercury and Gotham

ISBN: 978-0-7643-5360-4

Printed in the United States of America

Published by Schiffer Publishing, Ltd.
4880 Lower Valley Road
Atglen, PA 19310
Phone: (610) 593-1777; Fax: (610) 593-2002
E-mail: Info@schifferbooks.com
Web: www.schifferbooks.com

For our complete selection of fine books on this and related subjects, please visit our website at www.schifferbooks.com. You may also write for a free catalog.

Schiffer Publishing's titles are available at special discounts for bulk purchases for sales promotions or premiums. Special editions, including personalized covers, corporate imprints, and excerpts, can be created in large quantities for special needs. For more information, contact the publisher.

We are always looking for people to write books on new and related subjects. If you have an idea for a book, please contact us at proposals@schifferbooks.com.

"We started the DC Eagle Cam Project with the simple hope
of educating Americans about bald eagles, but the project ended up
teaching and inspiring people all over the world!"

— Al Cecere, Founder and President, *American Eagle Foundation*

For Al Cecere and Challenger

Al Cecere is founder and president of the American Eagle Foundation (AEF), a 501(c)(3) not-for-profit organization founded in 1985. AEF is dedicated to protecting and caring for the majestic bald eagle and other birds of prey. Challenger, a non-releasable bald eagle in the care of the American Eagle Foundation, serves as an educational ambassador for his species to help raise public awareness about America's living symbol of freedom. Challenger is the first bald eagle in US history trained to free-fly during the presentation of "The Star-Spangled Banner" at sporting and other major events in stadiums and arenas. Read more about Al, Challenger, and the American Eagle Foundation at www.eagles.org.

Al Cecere with Challenger.
Courtesy of Richard Suter Photography

Contents

Challenger, the free-flying bald eagle. © *Teena Ruark Gorrow*

Foreword

It all started back in the 1980s when my dad, Al Louis Cecere, saw a horrific newspaper photograph showing two dozen bald eagles laying side-by-side that had been shot and killed by poachers in the Dakotas. From that moment on, he wanted to become a "point of light" and dedicate his life to saving eagles. From his kitchen table in Nashville, Tennessee, he started a charity named the National Foundation to Protect America's Eagles and began to raise money to help eagles by standing in front of

Al Cecere along with daughters Julia Cecere (left) and Laura Serbens (right) band an approximately six-week-old eaglet that was hatched and raised by a non-releasable bald eagle breeding pair housed at the American Eagle Foundation. *Courtesy of the American Eagle Foundation*

AEF raptor facility. *Courtesy of John D. Prickett*

Eaglet being released from hack. *Courtesy of the American Eagle Foundation*

Eaglet in captivity. *Courtesy of the American Eagle Foundation*

Walmart stores with donation canisters. He later changed the name of the charity to the American Eagle Foundation, or AEF for short. More than thirty years later, the AEF has become one of the most widely recognized eagle and raptor conservation organizations in the United States.

At our raptor facility in Pigeon Forge, Tennessee, we provide a forever home to many eagles and other birds of prey that can't be released into the wild because they have permanent physical or mental disabilities. We provide them with daily care, feeding, and training, and many of the birds are used to educate children and adults at our Wings of America Birds of Prey show at Dollywood (Dolly Parton's theme park), school programs, veterans' homes, and special events coast to coast. Many of our eagles live in a large, naturally landscaped aviary at Dollywood called Eagle Mountain Sanctuary.

We also take in injured eagles and raptors. We rehabilitate them so that they can be released back into the wild.

Lastly, we care for several permanently disabled, non-releasable bald eagle breeding pairs that hatch and raise baby eagles, called eaglets, in captivity. Rather than having wild nests, they live in large aviaries with man-made nest boxes. When their eaglets are big enough, we take them to a hack tower, or artificial nesting tower, overlooking a lake, where they grow to full size and are released into the wild at about thirteen weeks of age.

Among our many resident raptors is a very special bald eagle named Challenger. This eagle was accidentally human-imprinted at about five weeks of age after falling out of his wild Louisiana nest. He was found and raised by well-meaning people. Because of his close interaction with humans as a nestling, Challenger began to think he was a person and never learned how to hunt. He was released into the wild twice but kept going near people to beg for food. Eventually, he was handed over to the AEF for permanent care.

Al Cecere and Challenger. *Courtesy of Jeff Jacobsen*

Challenger flies on 9-11 at M&T Bank Stadium, home of the Baltimore Ravens. © *Teena Ruark Gorrow*

Then my dad came up with an unprecedented idea. He wanted to see if this special, physically perfect eagle could be trained to free-fly through fan-filled sport stadiums while "The Star-Spangled Banner" was performed. So that's exactly what he and the AEF staff did. Challenger became the first eagle in US history to do this and has performed free-flight demonstrations at over 400 sporting games and other events across the United States. He has become a famous educational eagle ambassador.

In 2015, my dad and I were visiting Washington, DC, with Challenger and talking to members of Congress on Capitol Hill about American Eagle Day—a special day to celebrate eagles that my dad has been promoting for a number of years. Meanwhile, our friend Bob told us that a wild eagle pair had recently built a nest at the US National Arboretum. Naturally, we decided to pay a visit.

There we met a knowledgeable agricultural scientist named Sue who had been watching the eagles all year. She took us to look at the nest from afar. We told her that we had video cameras and microphones on eagle nests in Tennessee and Florida and mentioned how exciting it would be to have live-streaming video cameras on this unique nest, too. Being able to watch our national symbol living in our nation's capital . . . how cool would that be?

The rest is history.

Several official partners and other people joined the AEF in bringing the DC Eagle Cam Project to life, allowing Internet viewers to watch the daily activities of Mr. President and The First Lady twenty-four hours a day, seven days a week, and in high definition. It quickly

became one of the most popular live animal video cams on the Internet and was viewed by millions of people all over the world!

It has been an honor and privilege to be part of this project. As you explore this beautiful book featuring the life of Mr. President and The First Lady and their eaglets, we hope you will gain better insight into the magnificent and wonderful world of eagles.

And remember, if my dad could start saving eagles with just pennies and a passionate dream, imagine what *you* could do if you put your heart and mind to it.

— Julia Cecere,
Publicity, Marketing, and Social Media Manager
American Eagle Foundation, www.eagles.org
September 19, 2016

Acknowledgments

We lovingly acknowledge the Creator of birds and our precious family members including Wayne Gorrow, Paul and Ellen Ruark, Ernie Beath, Pam Koppie, and Tony and Nancy Koppie. We extend our heartfelt appreciation to Al Cecere, Julia Cecere, and the American Eagle Foundation for the opportunity to document the story of Mr. President and The First Lady, whose daily lives were live-streamed 24/7 to the masses through the DC Eagle Cam Project. We respectfully recognize the partnership between the American Eagle Foundation and US Department of Agriculture in cooperation with the US National Arboretum, Agricultural Research Service, Alfred State SUNY College of Technology, Department of Energy & Environment, US Fish & Wildlife Service, Piksel, and Friends of the National Arboretum. We also recognize the National Park Service and US Park Police, Aviation Unit.

Many people have worked behind the scenes to bring the DC Eagle Cam Project to the public. We gratefully acknowledge the following special people and organizations: Al Cecere, Julia Cecere, Spencer Williams, Laura

Sterbens, Patty Fernandez, Crystal Slusher, Carolyn Stalcup, Carol Caesar, Cathy Poer, MarthaAnn Madigan, Jodi Stelter, Sue Yingst, Marianne Wilson, Peggy Bryan, and Kim Rexroat from the American Eagle Foundation 2016 DC Eagle Cam Team; Michael Stalcup from Stringweb; Rob Colletti, Sarah Spradlin, Alan Riley, and other staff from Piksel; Sue Greeley, Ramon Jordan, Richard Olsen, Stefanye Washington, Mike Blum, Lou Webber, Dr. Chavonda Jacobs-Young, Sharon Durham, and Christopher Bentley from the US National Arboretum and US Department of Agriculture; Thomas Costello from the Friends of the National Arboretum; Dan Rauch, Tommy Wells, and Julia Christian from the DC Department of Energy & Environment; Jeffrey Stevens, Brad Thompson, Sean Kelly, Ethan Yanda, Thomas Wzientek, Justin King, Oliver Jackson, and Mike Lee from Alfred State SUNY College of Technology; Mike Cotter and Excel Tree Experts; Doug LaFortune with Treewise Consulting LLC; Nick Vichas and Mandy Glass with Apex Electric, Inc.; and Axis Communications. We also recognize Dolly Parton and Dollywood for supporting the vision of the American Eagle Foundation for many years and helping to make their eagle conservation work possible.

We offer sincere appreciation to the American Eagle Foundation staff and volunteers listed above, Sue Greeley, Dan Rauch, and Jeffrey Stevens for capturing and providing images from the AEF's live-streaming cameras. We gratefully acknowledge Sue Greeley and Dan Rauch for also generously sharing photographs they captured around the eagles' nesting and foraging territory. We thank Pete Schiffer, Cheryl Weber, Matthew Goodman, and the team at Schiffer Publishing for publishing the uplifting story about Mr. President and The First Lady.

Introduction

In 2014, a pair of mated bald eagles chose the most idyllic of nest sites within the nation's capital, Washington, DC, high in a tulip poplar tree among the Azalea Collection at the US National Arboretum. Then, in 2015, the American Eagle Foundation placed two high-definition video cameras above this nest and streamed the everyday lives of this bald eagle family to the world. The result: one of the most popular live animal cams on the Internet.

— *American Eagle Foundation*

Images 1–15 represent the 2016 nesting season of the DC Eagle Cam Project.

Chapter One
From the Beginning

One spring day, an American bald eagle soars high in the blue sky above Washington, DC. With outstretched wings, he floats over the nation's capital. It seems like the large raptor could drift forever on the wind currents and thermals without flapping his wings.

Courtesy of Dan Rauch/DOEE

Aerial view of Northeast Washington, DC. *Courtesy of Craig A. Koppie/USFWS*

Courtesy of Craig A. Koppie/USFWS

The eagle hovers over the Anacostia River. Suddenly, he dives toward the water and snatches a catfish with his powerful feet. Using his talons to grip the fish, the eagle flies toward a neighboring tree. He lands on a branch to eat his catch. He spends the rest of the day at home along the river.

Courtesy of Dan Rauch/DOEE

© Teena Ruark Gorrow

Aerial view of Kingman Island and the Anacostia River.
Courtesy of Craig A. Koppie/USFWS

As the sky turns orange around the setting sun, the eagle flies to nearby Kingman Island. There, he roosts alone for the night on a tall sycamore tree.

Months pass. Each day, this American symbol patrols the capital's skies and rivers. He often fishes the Anacostia. Sometimes he forages waterfowl or small mammals. At sunset, he returns to roost alone on Kingman Island.

Bald eagle concentration area. (Circles highlight eagles on branches.) © *Teena Ruark Gorrow*

In early fall, other bald eagles migrate through the Mid-Atlantic region. They stop in eagle concentration areas around the Chesapeake Bay watershed. The male eagle finds a female who will soon become his mate.

© Teena Ruark Gorrow

© Teena Ruark Gorrow

The male and female eagles conduct a bonding flight. *Courtesy of Dan Rauch/DOEE*

Aerial view of the US National Arboretum. *Courtesy of Craig A. Koppie/USFWS*

The eagle perches in a favorite foraging area. (A circle was added to show the eagle location.) *Courtesy of Dan Rauch/DOEE*

Over the next few weeks, the two eagles get to know each other. They conduct bonding flights above the capital city. With outstretched wings, the magnificent raptors glide across the sky like mirror images. They perch and roost along the Anacostia River. The eagles drift over the lovely forests and gardens at the US National Arboretum (USNA).

Before long, the two bald eagles become a bonded pair. They claim this territory and chase away other eagles. The male eagle no longer roosts alone at sunset.

Courtesy of Craig A. Koppie/USFWS

Courtesy of Dan Rauch/DOEE

In November, the eagles start carrying sticks to the top of a tulip poplar tree at the USNA. Standing about 100 feet tall, the tree's long limbs reach high into the sky. It is on a beautifully landscaped hillside in the arboretum's Azalea Collection.

By the end of January, the nest looks like a huge wooden bowl sitting atop the tulip poplar. One eagle stays on the nest at all times. The other eagle delivers food. These are signs that the female eagle has laid at least one egg.

A raptor biologist with the US Fish & Wildlife Service and a biologist with the National Park Service fly high over the eagle nest in a helicopter with the US Park Police. The experts, conducting an eagle nest survey along the DC corridor, are careful not to disturb the bird family. Using special zoom lenses, the biologists check the nest.

The biologists confirm that the eagle pair has one chick. Arboretum workers are pleased with this good news. Bald eagles have not nested on the grounds of the arboretum since 1947.

Courtesy of Dan Rauch/DOEE

(A circle was added to show the eagle nest.) *Courtesy of Craig A. Koppie/USFWS*

As the weeks pass, the chick grows as large as its parents. In early June, the adult-sized eaglet fledges from the nest. It perches on nearby trees and flies over the USNA.

Courtesy of Dan Rauch/DOEE

Courtesy of Dan Rauch/DOEE

The successful eagle nest story makes news headlines in the nation's capital. Although now recovered and no longer an endangered species, the bald eagle was once almost extinct. With the help of scientists and conservationists, eagles have returned to Washington, DC, and other cities across the US.

Courtesy of Dan Rauch/DOEE

Courtesy of Dan Rauch/DOEE

Even so, there are only two other known eagle pairs nesting in DC. Employees at the arboretum are excited that bald eagles have chosen a habitat within their protective fences.

Meanwhile, representatives from the American Eagle Foundation (AEF) have traveled to Capitol Hill with Challenger, their celebrity, non-releasable bald eagle. AEF, a not-for-profit organization, is dedicated to protecting bald eagles and other birds of prey. Upon hearing about the new eagle nest, they decide to visit the USNA before heading home to Tennessee. AEF has experience with installing and live-streaming cameras on eagles' nests for educational and research purposes in Tennessee and Florida. They talk with arboretum leadership about launching a live eagle nest cam project here.

Challenger visits Capitol Hill. *Courtesy of the American Eagle Foundation*

Courtesy of the American Eagle Foundation

The US National Arboretum and American Eagle Foundation form a partnership. They decide to place two cameras above the nest at the top of the tulip poplar tree. The cams will allow Internet users to see inside the eagle nest by visiting AEF's website at www.eagles.org.

Toward the end of summer, after the first breeding season ends and the eagle family leaves the area, the technical work begins at the tree. Trenches are dug for

Courtesy of the American Eagle Foundation

Courtesy of the American Eagle Foundation

Courtesy of the American Eagle Foundation

cables and state-of-the-art technology is installed. Two cameras are mounted on opposite tree limbs with low-power infrared lighting. This will allow twenty-four-hour nest viewing, but the nest will still look dark at night to the eagles. The cameras are connected to the Internet by a half-mile of fiber optic cable. To power the system, a mobile solar array is installed. The effort is named the DC Eagle Cam Project.

The video cam installation is complete and the nest cams are ready for use. But bald eagles do not always return to their first nesting site. Sometimes they build an alternative nest in the same territory. Everyone involved with the DC Eagle Cam Project must now wait to see if the eagles will return for a second breeding season.

Chapter Two
Meet Mr. President and The First Lady

The First Lady.

The First Lady (in the nest) and Mr. President survey their territory.

Mr. President perches on a nearby tree. Courtesy of Dan Rauch/DOEE

Eagles living in the wild are not usually named by humans. But if the eagle couple returns to their nest at the US National Arboretum, they will likely be viewed by millions of people watching the video cams operated by American Eagle Foundation staff and volunteers. And so in anticipation of their return, the eagles are given names. Because bald eagles are America's symbol and this nest is just a few miles from the White House, the male eagle is named Mr. President, and the female is named The First Lady.

At first glance, it is easy to recognize Mr. President and The First Lady as adult American bald eagles. Their wing and body feathers are almost all brown. Their head and tail feathers are mostly white. Both eagles have yellow, curved beaks pointing downward to a sharp tip.

However, there are slight differences in their appearance. A closer look at plumage patterns, beaks, and size can help identify which eagle is Mr. President and which is The First Lady.

How to Spot The First Lady

- Her brown feathers are lighter in color at the tips than those of Mr. President.
- Her beak is slightly darker at the tip than at the top.
- Her beak has a slight curve with a few indentations above the nares.
- She is larger than Mr. President.

How to Spot Mr. President

- His brown feathers are darker than those of The First Lady.
- His beak is a brighter shade of yellow and is straighter than The First Lady's beak.
- A white blaze extending from his white head feathers down to his chest is sometimes visible.

Mr. President and The First Lady perch on a favorite branch.

The exact weights and measurements of Mr. President and The First Lady are not known. Eagles can measure about thirty inches from the top of the head to the tip of the tail, with a wingspan over six feet. They normally weigh between six and fourteen pounds. Northern US eagles are bigger than those in the southern US. In addition, female eagles are generally larger and weigh more than males living in the same region.

The eagles' yellow legs and feet are powerful. Each foot has four muscular toes. Three of the toes face forward and one faces backward. Each toe is equipped with a curved, sharp-tipped talon. This strong combination helps eagles snatch and grip prey and carry sticks to the nest.

An eagle's foot and talons are shown next to a human's hand. *Courtesy of the American Eagle Foundation*

Adult bald eagles have bright yellow eyes. With excellent vision, stronger than humans, they can look forward and sideways at the same time. Biologists believe that when flying, eagles can see small mammals more than a mile away and spot fish swimming near the water's surface.

Like humans, eagles have eyelids that close when they are asleep. Unlike humans, eagles have an inner eyelid known as a nictitating membrane. This see-through, colored eyelid protects the eagles' eyes and closes when they blink.

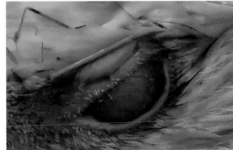

Nictitating membrane.

Each eye is framed by a fierce-looking yellow brow. Known as a supraorbital ridge, this bony structure acts like sunglasses to help the eagles hunt and fish in bright sunlight.

One sunny October morning, a bald eagle soars over the National Arboretum. It flies toward a forested hillside in the Azalea Collection. Landing on the familiar tulip poplar tree, the large raptor hops down into the nest. A second eagle follows with a stick clasped in its feet. This bird also lands on the tulip poplar. Mr. President and The First Lady have returned to their nest.

While she sizes up the nest, Mr. President surveys their territory. Turning his head from side to side, he observes the National Arboretum's grounds, the Anacostia River, and downtown Washington, DC. The two camouflaged video cameras installed above the nest do not seem to be a

Courtesy of Dan Rauch/DOEE

Mr. President and The First Lady have returned to their nest. *Photos courtesy of Sue Greeley/USNA*

Mr. President and The First Lady at home in their urban setting.

concern to either of the birds, just as the AEF and US Fish & Wildlife Service anticipated.

In a few months, Mr. President and The First Lady will prepare for their second nesting season. For now, the pair enjoys the autumn skies over the nation's capital. They soar high above the busy city. They glide along the rivers. They tour the forests and gardens at the arboretum. Guarding their breeding territory, they chase away other raptors including eagles entering their space. They perch and roost in favorite locations near the nest tree. The eagles are home again.

Chapter Three
Twigs, Sticks, and Nest Building

The US National Arboretum is a perfect place for Mr. President and The First Lady to nest. Here, they have tall, mature trees for nesting, perching, and roosting. The peaceful landscape provides an almost undisturbed setting away from the city's commotion.

The Anacostia River flows along the eastern edge of the arboretum. With its streams and creeks, the Anacostia travels into the Potomac River. Dozens of fish species live in these two rivers including catfish, bass, perch, and shad. Because an eagle's diet is eighty to ninety percent fish, the river will be a reliable food source. With the Anacostia in view from the tulip poplar, Mr. President and The First Lady can fish close to the nest.

Courtesy of Dan Rauch/DOEE

Aerial view of the US National Arboretum. *Courtesy of Craig A. Koppie/USFWS*

It takes a lot of fish to feed a growing family of eaglets. In addition to fish, bald eagles eat waterfowl like geese and ducks. They also eat small mammals including muskrats, squirrels, and rabbits. Sometimes eagles consume turtles or carrion. While Mr. President and The First Lady are known to forage for all of these, they also hunt groundhogs, especially when the river waters rise and become murky during rainy periods. The nearby fields and forests will provide additional areas to forage.

Mr. President.

The First Lady eats a catfish.

Depending on where eagles choose to breed in the US, their nesting territory and timeline of activities can vary. Even so, their basic needs are the same. Eagles require food, a nearby body of water, and safe shelter in an undisturbed area. At the US National Arboretum, Mr. President and The First Lady have found a good home.

Mr. President and The First Lady at the tulip poplar tree. *Photos above courtesy of Sue Greeley/USNA*

Nestorations begin.

During November, Mr. President and The First Lady visit their tulip poplar tree. They perch together inside the nest and adjust a few sticks. They perch on the tree's limbs beside the nest. The eagles might be deciding whether to repair this nest or build a new nest in a different tree. They will gradually add sticks and occasionally rest in the nest overnight.

In December, Mr. President and The First Lady carry sticks to their nest. Repairs, or "nestorations," are now underway. The eagle mates will raise their next brood of chicks at the National Arboretum.

The nest cams have not yet gone live to the masses. But the American Eagle Foundation and National Arboretum insiders watch as Mr. President and The First Lady create a cozy home for their second family.

Eagles usually return to the same nest year after year. Even so, additional twigs, branches, and grasses are needed to prepare the nest for a new family.

A typical eagle's nest is about five to six feet across and three to four feet high. It must be large enough to hold the

Aerial view of the nest belonging to Mr. President and The First Lady. *Courtesy of Craig A. Koppie/USFWS*

Eagle nests can become large and heavy when used for several years. *Courtesy of Craig A. Koppie/USFWS*

adults and their brood. The eaglets will grow as large as their parents before fledging at eleven to twelve weeks of age.

Nests can become very large and heavy when they are used for many years. In fact, one eagle nest was twelve feet deep and was estimated to weigh more than a ton.

Mr. President and The First Lady's nest in the tulip poplar tree is about five feet across and four feet high. As they bring additional branches, the nest will become larger. It is already wider and deeper than it was the previous year.

With their legs and feet, the eagles break dead branches from treetops. They also pick up sticks and twigs from the ground near the rivers and forests. Using their beaks and feet, the eagles arrange each stick and twig in place.

Stick size is usually between two and three feet long. But some branches are as long as four feet. Thicker branches, one half to one inch wide, are used for the nest's base, walls, and rails. Smaller sticks and twigs are used inside the nest and to fill the nest walls.

The dedicated eagles seem to agree on how to prepare their nest. They work side by side, often starting before sunrise. They replace fallen branches. They strengthen outer nest walls and rails. They use twigs and sticks to fill holes. Sometimes when Mr. President leaves the nest, The First Lady rearranges the sticks he put into place. Perhaps she is in charge of their tree house.

The eagles add dried grasses, leaves, straw, moss, and pine needles to the nest. Using their beaks, they scatter these softer items over the crisscrossed sticks. Near the center, they form a soft nest cup or bowl where the eggs will be laid and incubated. This will make comfortable bedding once the eaglets are hatched and brooded by their parents.

In early January, Mr. President and The First Lady sit on the nest as if to test the cup. They adjust a few twigs and fluff the grasses. They continue strengthening the nest with branches. Soon, it will be time to lay the eggs.

Chapter Four

Eggs!

Mated eagles cartwheel through the air. *Photos © Teena Ruark Gorrow*

Mr. President and The First Lady sky-dance. *Courtesy of Dan Rauch/DOEE*

With their nest almost ready, Mr. President and The First Lady know it is time to start their family. They meet high in the sky for courtship flights. In perfect harmony, they dance through the air in a majestic soaring fashion. Wing-to-wing, they glide. They fly in circles while he chases her. Suddenly, they lock their feet together. Connected, they cartwheel through the air in a free fall. Just before reaching the ground, the eagles unlock their feet. They soar upward for another sky-dance. The eagles mate inside their nest and while perched on nearby tree branches.

Mr. President and The First Lady mate.

During the afternoon on February 10, The First Lady lays an egg. The white, oval egg measures about three inches long.

Sometimes eagles begin incubating their eggs immediately. Other times, eagles delay incubation until all eggs have been laid. The First Lady and Mr. President sometimes leave this first egg exposed to the cool weather.

Perhaps the experienced parents intend to lay more eggs. Scientists suggest that delayed incubation can help postpone hatching and allow eggs to hatch one to two days apart. When chicks are closer in age, there is usually less sibling rivalry and less competition for food. Leaving the first egg uncovered could help it hatch around the same time as other eggs The First Lady will lay.

On February 12, The First Lady begins to fully incubate the egg. She carefully lowers her body over the nest cup and gently rocks back and forth. With a quick shake, she fluffs her feathers. The plumage on the lower part of her body helps cover the cup like a blanket. She sits still with her brood patch resting on top of the egg.

The brood patch is an area of almost featherless skin near an eagle's abdomen. It is used to apply body heat while sitting on a clutch of eggs and to keep hatched eaglets warm.

Using her beak, she tucks grass around the egg and between her body and the nest. This helps prevent drafts of air from blowing into the nest cup.

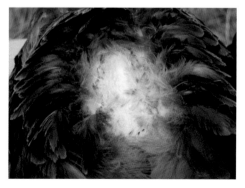

An eagle's brood patch. © *Craig A. Koppie*

Every now and then, The First Lady stands. She uses her beak and feet to gently turn the egg. Egg-turning prevents the unborn chick from sticking to the inside of its shell. It also helps the egg and chick to stay evenly warmed. The large parent eagle is careful not to step on the egg with her powerful feet, or puncture it with her sharp talons.

Like other female eagles, The First Lady does most of the incubating. When she is ready to stretch her wings, Mr. President takes over the incubation duties. Once he settles over the nest cup, The First Lady takes a break or goes to forage.

Bald eagles lay their eggs one at a time and typically two to three days apart. They usually lay a clutch of one to three eggs during their annual nesting season. Only time will tell how many eggs there will be this season.

Courtesy of Dan Rauch/DOEE

Courtesy of Dan Rauch/DOEE

If all goes well, the egg should hatch after about thirty-five days of incubation. Until then, Mr. President and The First Lady keep their unhatched egg safe, warm, and dry.

Now that egg-laying has started, there is a lot of work to do around the nest. Mr. President perches on nearby trees to guard the nest and nesting territory. He chases away potential predators like raccoons and other raptors including eagles. He brings sticks and grasses to maintain the nest. Mr. President also forages prey and delivers meals to The First Lady.

On the morning of February 14, The First Lady lays a second egg. Mr. President and The First Lady now have a clutch of two eggs.

The next day, the American Eagle Foundation begins to stream the video cams live on its website. AEF sends out alerts and press releases to the national media. Soon, people across the country and around the world are talking about the DC Eagle Cam Project.

Unaware that hundreds of thousands of people are watching them online, the experienced parents protect their eggs and territory. Over the next few weeks, they take turns incubating the eggs. They guard the nest from predators. Using their bodies, they shield the eggs from pounding rain, sleet, and snow. Wintry winds rock the tree and nest, but the eggs stay safe, dry, and warm.

Mr. President and The First Lady switch places during incubation.

Mr. President and The First Lady are extremely dedicated and attentive to their unhatched chicks. Day after day and night after night, they protect their eggs. As mid-March approaches, hatching could start at any time.

Chapter Five
Hatching to Fledging

On the evening of March 16, light tapping begins inside the shell of the first egg. Using the egg tooth on the end of its tiny beak, the eagle chick has started pecking its shell. The hatching process has begun just thirty-five days after the first egg was laid.

The next morning, Mr. President and The First Lady continue incubating the eggs. When switching places, the parents-to-be watch their little eaglet begin to emerge from its egg.

As the pipping continues, a small hole begins to form. Soon, Mr. President and The First Lady can see the eaglet's beak.

For more than a day, the eagle chick works to break free. There is stillness while the little bird rests and then the tapping starts again. Finally, the shell fractures. A tired eaglet hatches on March 18 at 8:27 a.m. from the first egg.

Weighing just a few ounces, the hatchling is not strong enough to hold up its head. The petite raptor looks like a ball of grayish fluff. Light gray down covers most of its body and wings. Darker-colored down surrounds its closed eyes.

Near the top of the little curved beak are nares for breathing. The egg tooth, which was used to break out of the shell, is at the beak's tip. This will eventually be absorbed as the beak grows to full size.

The eaglet has a small, dark ear opening on each side of its head for hearing that is covered by down. Two rubbery feet are hidden from view. Each tiny foot has four toes with talons.

The little eaglet is tired, weak, and helpless. Its down is still damp from living inside the egg. It sleeps beside the unhatched egg in the cozy nest cup. The First Lady gently lowers her body over the hatchling and egg. Her warmth provides shelter from the chilly March air and helps dry the baby's down feathers. At this stage, the eaglet is unable to control its own body temperature and relies on a parent for warmth. As the nestling sleeps, the mother adjusts grasses and tidies the nest cup. She eats pieces of the hatchling's broken eggshell.

Before long, the hatchling begins to stir under The First Lady's breast feathers. Now awake, the little eaglet is hungry and chirping. The mother knows it is time for the baby's first meal.

Earlier, Mr. President delivered a fish to the nest. The First Lady stands to feed the eaglet. She tears away a bone-free bite of fish with her beak. Gently, she leans toward the hatchling's tiny head. Still tired and weak, the nestling is wobbly.

The First Lady offers a small piece of the fish. The chick moves toward its mother, but misses the pass. The eaglet's eyes will not be sharply focused for a few days. Although the first feeding was not perfect, the nestling eventually gets a taste of the fish. The mother tucks the eaglet back under her brood patch along with the second egg to keep them warm.

Mr. President and The First Lady keep close watch on their new arrival. They are careful not to step on the little hatchling or poke the egg with their sharp talons.

The chick sleeps peacefully against the unhatched egg. Several times throughout the day, the parents offer small bites of bone-free fish. The nestling seems ready to eat and opens its beak to accept the food. The eaglet will gradually learn to grab and swallow its food without dropping a bite.

Soon there is more excitement at the nest. On the morning of March 19, Mr. President and The First Lady see that their second egg is starting to hatch. The pipping has produced a chip, or pip, in the eggshell.

The First Lady checks on the egg while feeding the nestling. There is tapping from inside the shell. It will take a while for the chick to break free. Mr. President perches on a limb slightly above the nest. The First Lady broods the chick and incubates the egg.

The little eaglet works hour after hour to break free from its shell. About 3:00 a.m. on March 20, the first nestling has a little sister or brother. The second egg has now hatched.

Two nestlings snuggle in the egg cup's soft grasses. The helpless eaglets are barely able to hold up their heads. Even so, both chicks will eventually grow as large as their parents.

These tiny raptors will one day stand about two feet tall. Their wobbly feet will be strong and adult-sized. When grown to full size, dark feathers will replace the soft, puffy, grayish down feathers now covering their little bodies. Petite wings will develop into a wingspan measuring six feet or more. In eleven to twelve weeks, the eaglets will take flight from their parents' cozy nest. From hatching to fledging, their transformation will be an amazing journey.

Mr. President and The First Lady both leave the nest for a few minutes. Perhaps they are protecting their territory from an intruder. The eaglets bop their little heads around as if looking for their parents.

Day and night, the dedicated parents take care of their chicks. They know how to feed, warm, and protect their little ones.

The parents also take care of each other. On this sunny March afternoon, Mr. President feeds fish to The First Lady.

The eagle family members are unaware of their fame, but millions of people are watching through the DC Eagle Cam Project. The viewers are amazed by the hatching, feeding, nurturing ways of the parents, and rapid growth of the eaglets.

Because the eagle mates have names, it is decided that the eaglets should also have names. For now, the older chick will be called DC2. The younger eaglet will be named DC3.

DC stands for the DC eagle cam nest. The number refers to the order in which the eggs hatched. DC1 is the name of the eaglet that hatched during the mated pair's first breeding season. DC2 is the eagle parents' second chick, but the first to hatch this season.

Now March 23, the nestlings are growing in size and strength. By chirping, they tell their mother that two hungry eaglets are waiting for food. The First Lady is happy to offer another meal. She responds by gently presenting small pieces of fish with her large beak. The chicks eagerly accept the food brought down to their little beaks.

Both parents keep watch over their eaglets and maintain a presence at the nest. Day and night, Mr. President and The First Lady are never far from their young.

The First Lady examines the fish beside her sleeping eaglets. It is time for another feeding. After a tasty treat, the nestlings cuddle inside the nest cup for their next of many naps.

Mr. President and The First Lady work around the clock caring for their nestlings. They provide warmth, protection, and food.

As March comes to a close, the eaglets are thriving. They are larger and appear stronger as they scoot around the nest cup. The cup's walls provide a warm, cozy, and protective environment. The eaglets will stay in this area until they are strong enough to move out of the cup.

At two weeks old, DC2 and DC3 can sit upright and hold up their heads for longer periods of time. The young eaglets are more mobile but not yet able to fully stand or walk. To move around the nest cup, they scoot or use their tarsi to crawl. They often plop down on their bellies and heads. They've discovered that their parents make a good leaning post.

Between fourteen and eighteen days old, the eaglets have a growth spurt. They appear to have doubled in size with a larger head, body, feet, and wings. Light grayish-colored down feathers now have a darker gray appearance. The egg tooth is still evident but will eventually be absorbed into the upper part of the beak. Besides sleeping and eating, they play with twigs and other objects in the nest. They also groom their down feathers.

The soft nest grasses make a comfortable bed for the eaglets and their parents. Mr. President and The First Lady snooze, too.

Mr. President delivers prey several times each day to the three-week-old nestlings. The First Lady also hunts and brings food to the nest. She can carry even larger prey to the nest since she is larger than her mate. It takes more and more food to satisfy these growing youngsters. Sibling rivalry can be a concern when there is not enough food. But because there is plenty of food in this nest, the siblings are not fighting over pieces of fish. In fact, DC2 and DC3 often snuggle with each other.

The eaglets' first pinfeathers are now easily seen on their wings. Over the next several weeks, the tips will grow into full-length flight feathers. Their feet are also noticeably larger.

The eaglets' lighter gray down feathers are changing to a darker gray. The down's texture, which looks like lamb's wool, provides insulation. This means that the eaglets can control body temperature without being brooded by their parents.

From time to time, The First Lady rearranges nest grasses and straw. This keeps the nest comfortable for both the adults and the babies. She also uses grass to patch empty spots and cover prey remains for future feedings.

DC2 and DC3 are experiencing warm mid-April days in the nation's capital. As the sun beats down on their nest, the young eaglets can feel overheated due to the insulation of their down.

To release body heat, the four-week-old nestlings pant with mouths wide open and sometimes spread their wings. They also huddle in the shade of the tree. At times, they look for shade in front of their parents.

Thirty-two to thirty-four days after hatching, the eaglets are continuing to develop. Dark brown body feathers show through the down feathers. Bone and muscle development help them stand, stretch, and "winger-cize," or exercise their wings.

Having outgrown their nest cup, the chicks now wander over the full area of the nest to explore. The nest cup is no longer needed or visible.

Between five and six weeks old, DC2 and DC3 are alert and watching the world around them. They are able to stand and walk across the nest platform. Their tail feathers, now protruding noticeably, help with balance.

© Teena Ruark Gorrow

Courtesy of the American Eagle Foundation

While the eagles watch the world around their nest, millions of people around the globe are watching them. As April draws to a close, Mr. President, The First Lady, and their nestlings have received more than thirty-five million views from 100 countries at www.dceaglecam.org.

Through social media, nest cam fans have been voting to rename the famous Internet eaglets. In a ceremony at the US National Arboretum near Capitol Hill, the nestlings' new names are unveiled. The eaglet known as DC2 is now Freedom. DC3's new name is Liberty.

Seven-week-old Freedom and Liberty are growing and appear to be doing well. Their plumage is now a dark shade of brown.

During May, some days in the capital city are hot and sunny, while others are cool and windy. This year, there are a lot of rainy days. Rain can be a relief from the spring's heat for the eagle family. The rain also helps remove dirt and grime from their feathers.

The siblings are like mirror images. Size is still the best way to tell the birds apart: Freedom is slightly larger than Liberty, and possibly a female.

The eaglets are growing rapidly and are now about eight weeks old. They can add almost a half-pound of body weight each week until reaching nine or ten weeks old. Their tail feathers, not yet fully grown, are five to six inches long.

Active and energetic, Freedom and Liberty look for things to do inside the nest. They play with sticks, jump, hop, and flap their wings. Hopping helps build leg muscles. Winger-cizing helps build wing muscles.

Suddenly, Freedom "branches" onto a tree limb slightly above the nest. Later that morning, Liberty does the same.

The active eaglets also need sleep. To settle down for a nap, Freedom and Liberty place their heads on their backs the way their parents sleep. Then, they nuzzle their beaks into their back feathers. This position helps the birds conserve heat and rests their neck muscles.

Freedom and Liberty awaken. Using their beaks, they take a moment to bond. Shortly after, they have an early morning workout.

Liberty mantles a fish brought to the nest by Mr. President. At sixty-one days old, the eaglet has learned an important survival skill. But Freedom is also interested in the fish. It is settled when The First Lady takes control and divides it between the two hungry siblings.

A rainy morning at the nest.

There is little room to spare when Mr. President, The First Lady, Freedom, and Liberty are all in the nest at the same time. Now over ten weeks old, the eaglets observe their parents more closely. They are keenly interested in all activity around the nest.

On June 3, Freedom begins wing-flapping with fierce determination. Gaining confidence, the brave bird releases its grip on the nest while flapping. For a moment, the eaglet is airborne. Freedom then hops onto a tree limb and poses with outstretched wings. The young raptor might be imagining what it will feel like to fly.

After a while, Freedom continues flapping excitedly across the nest. With tail feathers fully extended, the eaglet "hop-flaps" from one side of the nest to the other. Liberty closely watches the older sibling. Freedom lands on a limb, but then switches spots to perch on the opposite branch.

In their eleventh week since hatching, the eaglets are now fully grown. They look out over the landscape, including the arboretum grounds and perhaps downtown Washington, DC. They could be studying the landmarks.

They could even be considering a flight plan. Whatever their thoughts, both birds seem ready for their first flight and will soon fledge from the nest.

Two sleeping babies snuggle in their nest on the morning of June 5. Maybe they are having sweet dreams about flying.

Later that morning, Freedom looks out over the horizon. The eaglet bobs its head and positions its wings tightly against its body. Liberty watches as Freedom prepares for take-off. It is time. Freedom has initiated a launching procedure.

Quickly, the eaglet springs from the safety of the nest's rim. Freedom is flying! Just eleven weeks and two days after hatching, Mr. President and The First Lady's older chick has officially fledged.

Completing the first flight and landing can be tricky. DC Eagle Cam fans watch closely, eager to see if Freedom is safe. The fledgling is spotted while landing in a tree across from the nest. Success!

The siblings interact when Freedom returns to the nest.

A while later, Freedom returns to the nest. One can only imagine how Freedom communicates the first flight experience to Liberty.

Courtesy of Sue Greeley/USNA

Freedom explores territory around the tulip poplar homestead. The fledgling soars above the nesting site and perches in nearby trees, gradually getting to know the area. One favorite perching location is a tree directly across from the nest. Mr. President and The First Lady closely monitor Freedom's activity.

Liberty also watches Freedom's every move. The younger sibling, thought to be a male, is perching higher and higher on branches above the nest. Liberty's turn to fly free will soon come.

Freedom (white circle) perches in a tree directly across from the nest (yellow circle), while Liberty perches on a branch (red circle) above the nest.

Courtesy of Sue Greeley/USNA

On June 9, four days after Freedom fledged, the eaglets enjoy the view of downtown DC. While Freedom sits on a branch, Liberty perches on one of the nest cams. Then Liberty changes spots to perch near Freedom on the branch.

With wings spread, Liberty suddenly leans forward. Three seconds later, the eaglet is airborne. Eleven weeks and four days after hatching, Mr. President and The First Lady's youngest chick has fledged. Liberty is flying!

Now that both eaglets have fledged, DC Eagle Cam fans sometimes see an empty nest on their computer monitors. Although they

Mr. President (left) and Liberty perch on a branch west of their nest tree at the US National Arboretum.
Courtesy of Sue Greeley/USNA

are out of view, Mr. President, The First Lady, Freedom, and Liberty are not far from the nest. They fly above the National Arboretum. They play and chase each other over the tree canopy. While the parents forage along the Anacostia, the juveniles practice gliding and landing. When it is time for a break, they perch in nearby trees.

© Craig A. Koppie

To the delight of cam fans, the eaglets are still spending time at the nest. The siblings often sit together inside the nest and perch on tree branches above and around the nest. The birds also visit the nest to devour food delivered by Mr. President and The First Lady.

The youngsters' food-begging cries to their parents can be heard over the arboretum hillside. Mr. President and The First Lady will bring meals to the nest for a few more weeks. But the amount of food is less now that the eaglets can fly. Biologists believe this encourages the fledglings to follow their parents to the river. There they will learn survival skills including how to fish on their own.

Food delivery by Mr. President. © *Craig A. Koppie*

Freedom and Liberty hop and jump along the nest tree's limbs. This play time is important for the siblings' growth and development. With each round, their bodies are getting stronger and their balance improves.

The siblings perform adorable eaglet antics. Since hatching, Freedom and Liberty have shared a close bond. They seem to enjoy each other's company and spend long periods of time perching next to each other at the nest tree.

© Craig A. Koppie

© Craig A. Koppie

© Craig A. Koppie

© Craig A. Koppie

© Craig A. Koppie

Freedom and Liberty always have something to do. They stretch their wings, feet, and tail feathers. They rub their beaks against tree limbs. They closely observe activity around the nest.

While people celebrate the Fourth of July holiday in the nation's capital, Freedom and Liberty perch together on a branch above their nest at the National Arboretum.

The siblings do not know that they are America's living symbol of freedom or that the DC Eagle Cam Project received over sixty-three million views during a five-month period. The eaglets are unaware that they inspired and educated the viewers who watched their transformation from hatchlings to fledglings. They just know that it is almost time to leave their home.

© Craig A. Koppie

Soon, Freedom and Liberty may journey south along the Potomac River. They may gather with other bald eagles known to congregate in the area before possibly heading toward the Chesapeake Bay.

But because Washington, DC, is imprinted in their memories, perhaps Freedom and Liberty will return one day as adults. Maybe they will each find a mate and raise families of their own. For now, DC Eagle Cam fans enjoy the final precious images of their darling eaglets as nesting season comes to a close.

Twigs and Tweets

A. The DC Eagle Cam Project

The DC Eagle Cam Project is a partnership between the American Eagle Foundation and the US Department of Agriculture, in cooperation with the US National Arboretum, Agricultural Research Service, Alfred State SUNY College of Technology, Department of Energy & Environment, US Fish & Wildlife Service, Piksel, and Friends of the National Arboretum.

In 2015, the AEF installed cameras, infrared lighting, and other equipment in and around the nest tree. The US National Arboretum ran a half-mile of fiber optic cable to the camera control station.

Donations marked DC Eagle Cam will be directed to the operational costs associated with the DC Eagle Cam and the AEF's Live Nest Cam Program. Visit www.eagles.org/donate, or send contributions to the American Eagle Foundation, PO Box 333, Pigeon Forge, TN 37868.

Courtesy of the American Eagle Foundation

The system is powered by a large mobile solar array containing several deep cycle batteries designed and built by students and staff from Alfred State SUNY College of Technology and partially funded by the Department of Energy & Environment. USNA installed a backup generator that will maintain power if inclement weather causes the solar array to become ineffective.

The high-definition streaming of the cameras is hosted, funded, and operated by the American Eagle Foundation on www.dceaglecam.org.

B. About the American Eagle Foundation

The American Eagle Foundation (AEF) is a 501(c)(3) nonprofit charitable organization whose mission is to care for and protect the USA's living symbol of freedom—the bald eagle—and other birds of prey through the four pillars of education, repopulation, conservation, and rehabilitation. The foundation is headquartered in the foothills of the Great Smoky Mountains, Pigeon Forge, Tennessee.

AEF headquarters. *Courtesy of John D. Prickett*

In 1985, the American Eagle Foundation began as a dream at the kitchen table of Al Cecere and was originally funded with money that volunteers collected in coin containers in front of Walmart stores in Nashville. Cecere had come across an Associated Press photo in a Tennessee newspaper depicting about two dozen dead bald eagles that had been shot by poachers in the Dakotas. After learning that bald eagles were on the brink of extinction in the lower forty-eight states, Cecere left his career in the entertainment production business and dedicated his life to restoring the bald eagle to America's lands, waterways, and skies, and to help "Build A Nest Egg" for their future care and protection.

In 1990, the AEF entered into a multi-year corporate partnership with the Dollywood Company to design and develop the United States Eagle Center at Dollywood in Pigeon Forge. This facility would be used to conduct public environmental education, daily care of non-releasable birds of prey, raptor rehabilitation, and a bald eagle breeding/release program.

Dolly Parton, Al Cecere, and Challenger. *Courtesy of the American Eagle Foundation*

Courtesy of the American Eagle Foundation

In April 1991, Dolly Parton, Al Cecere, and Bob Hope participated in the Grand Opening Ceremony for Eagle Mountain Sanctuary by releasing a permanently disabled bald eagle into the world's largest naturally landscaped eagle aviary. Today, the AEF has grown into an internationally recognized bald eagle conservation organization.

Education

The AEF's educational outreach ranges from the Wings of America Birds of Prey show at Dollywood, to educational programs at schools and veterans' care facilities across the United States, to appearances at professional and collegiate sporting events, as well as conventions, trade shows, and special events throughout the country. The organization has successfully performed tens of thousands of education programs since 1991 using non-releasable trained birds.

The Wings of America Birds of Prey show and Eagle Mountain Sanctuary bald eagle aviary at Dollywood have educated tens of millions of visitors from around the world about bald eagles and the importance of protecting and conserving the USA's living symbol of freedom.

Since 1995, the AEF's famous non-releasable, trained free-flying bald eagle, Challenger, has made hundreds of free-flight performances across the US at stadiums, arenas, and schools. The AEF conducts these educational programs and flights with the licensed permission of the US Fish & Wildlife Service and various state fish and wildlife agencies.

Repopulation

Since 1992, the AEF's captive-breeding and hacking programs have resulted in over 150 young bald eagles being set free into the foothills of the Great Smoky Mountains in East Tennessee from an artificial nesting tower. Most of these eaglets have come from the AEF's non-releasable bald eagle breeding pairs (who choose each other

Courtesy of John D. Prickett

Courtesy of John D. Prickett

as mates in captivity), while the others have been trans-ferred to the AEF from zoos, raptor facilities, and wild nests around the country. The AEF has also released nearly a dozen golden eaglets into the wild, most of which were hatched by the AEF's non-releasable golden eagle breeding pair. Since the early 1980s, the AEF has been a partner in releasing nearly 400 translocated and cap-tive-hatched bald eaglets into the wilds of Tennessee in cooperation with the Tennessee Wildlife Resources Agency and US Fish & Wildlife Service.

Conservation

The AEF cares for a large collection of seventy to eighty non-releasable raptors and other birds daily, including the world's largest collection of non-releasable bald eagles, most of which reside inside Eagle Mountain Sanctuary aviary at Dollywood. These birds are non-releasable due to permanent physical disabilities or human imprinting/ socialization. The AEF supports bald eagle conservation around the country by issuing nearly $100,000 in bald eagle grants annually.

Rehabilitation

The AEF has rehabilitated hundreds of injured bald eagles and other birds of prey and released them back into the wild. If injuries are beyond repair, the birds are often given a permanent home at the AEF or another federally licensed raptor facility.

—*American Eagle Foundation*

C. About the US National Arboretum

© Craig A. Koppie

The National Capitol Columns now reside at the US National Arboretum. © Teena Ruark Gorrow

The US National Arboretum is a US Department of Agriculture research and education facility and a living museum. It is dedicated to serving the public and improving our environment by developing and promoting improved floral and landscape plants and new technologies through scientific research, educational programs, display gardens, and germplasm conservation. It is a national center for public education that welcomes visitors in a stimulating and aesthetically pleasing environment.

Established in 1927, the arboretum is part of the Agricultural Research Service (ARS), the principal in-house research arm of the US Department of Agriculture. ARS conducts research to develop and transfer solutions to agricultural problems of high national priority and provides information access and dissemination to ensure high-quality, safe food, and other agricultural products; to assess the nutritional needs of Americans; to sustain a competitive agricultural economy; to enhance the natural resource base and the environment; and to provide economic opportunities for rural citizens, communities, and society as a whole. For more information about ARS, visit www.ars.usda.gov.

—*Reprinted with permission from the US National Arboretum*

D. Challenger, the Free-Flying Bald Eagle

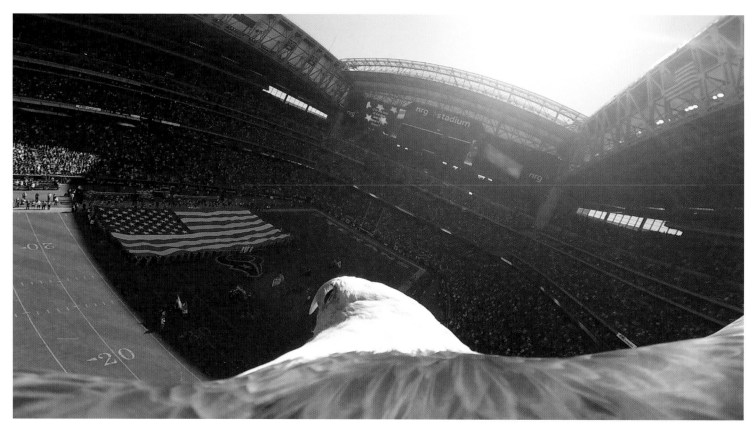

Courtesy of the American Eagle Foundation

The crowd erupts into a loud roar. Challenger, the bald eagle, spreads his wings and soars through the stadium as a soulful rendition of "The Star-Spangled Banner" is sung from the fifty-yard line. He swoops! He circles! He dives! Suddenly the crowd grows silent as he makes his final descent. As the last word of the national anthem resonates throughout the stadium, Challenger gracefully lands on his trainer's glove. Thousands cheer and wipe tears from their cheeks, touched by the sight of our living symbol of freedom soaring right before their eyes.

In the spring of 1989, a young bald eagle (about five weeks of age) was blown from a wild nest in Louisiana during a storm. Fortunately, he was rescued by some well-meaning people who proceeded to hand-feed and raise him. Unfortunately, he experienced too much human contact

Young Challenger. *Courtesy of the American Eagle Foundation*

Al Cecere shows Challenger to the crowd. *Courtesy of the American Eagle Foundation*

Challenger. *Courtesy of Laura Jacobsen*

at a very young age and became highly human-socialized.

Challenger's rescuers transferred Challenger to the Audubon Zoo of New Orleans. According to the records of the Alabama biologists, they picked up Challenger at the Audubon Zoo on June 8, 1989. At this time, they estimated his age to be about eight weeks. This means he most likely hatched between April 9 and 15, 1989 (the AEF celebrates Challenger's birthday each year around Earth Day). They delivered him to a hacking tower near Scottsboro, Alabama, for release into the wild when he was twelve to thirteen weeks old.

Challenger was released into the wild twice that summer and landed near people three different times in search of food. The first time was in Alabama near some fishermen and the second time was in a Little League baseball field in Iowa, where he was found emaciated. Challenger was transported back to wildlife officials, where he was fattened up and re-released. Once more, the young eagle landed near a man to beg for food, this time at Percy Priest Lake outside Nashville, Tennessee.

The man was frightened, picked up a stick, and was about to hit the eagle. Fortunately, another man intervened and prevented the bird from being harmed. This was the third time the eagle had sought out people to look for food when he became hungry. At that point, it was determined that he could not survive and hunt on his own in the wild. Federal and state fish and wildlife agencies placed the eagle under the care of the American Eagle

Challenger and Al Cecere during an event rehearsal. *Photos © Teena Ruark Gorrow*

Foundation, which was headquartered in the Nashville area at that time.

The AEF decided to name this eagle Challenger in honor of the fallen crew of the space shuttle. Challenger became well trained and was used to educate people about the importance of protecting his species.

Challenger was the first bald eagle in US history trained to free-fly into major sports stadiums, arenas, school auditoriums, and ballrooms during the presentation of the national anthem. Challenger's first indoor performance was the Bassmaster Classic in Greensboro, North Carolina, in 1995, but his first big outdoor stadium debut was at the 1996 Paralympic Games in Atlanta, Georgia. Some of his most noteworthy appearances since then include the WWII Memorial groundbreaking, NFL and MLB games across the US, and national TV shows including Dateline NBC, Fox and Friends, Good Morning America, the David Letterman Show, and Larry King Live. Challenger's image is on a Tennessee specialty license plate and on legal tender coins issued by the US Mint.

The American Eagle Foundation is blessed to have been entrusted with this magnificent eagle so many years ago. He has touched the lives of millions of Americans and continues to daily touch the lives of his handlers and others. Challenger is truly one-of-a-kind. There will never be another like him.

—*American Eagle Foundation*

Al Cecere and Challenger during a ceremony at the US National Arboretum when the DC Eagle Cam nestlings received their names.
© *Teena Ruark Gorrow*

E. American Bald Eagle Basics

- A large raptor, or bird of prey, found only in North America.
- Scientific name: *Haliaeetus leucocephalus*.
- Referred to as America's living symbol of freedom.
- Became America's national symbol when Congress adopted the Great Seal of the United States on June 20, 1782.
- Usually monogamous and mates for life.
- Adults generally weigh six to fourteen pounds, measure thirty to forty inches from head to tail, and have a wingspan of six to eight feet.
- Reaches full maturity at four to five years old with white head and tail feathers; also has yellow eyes, beak, and feet.
- Before four to five years old, feathers are mostly brown but might have some lighter/white mottling; eyes and beaks are also dark.
- Females are slightly larger than males.
- Life span in the wild is probably less than forty years. Eagles in captivity could live even longer, up to fifty years or more.

F. American Bald Eagle Symbolism

The bald eagle was selected as the US national emblem by the Second Continental Congress on June 20, 1782. For over 200 years, it has served as the pride of America's skies and the living symbol of all that Americans stand for: freedom, courage, strength, spirit, and excellence.

The bald eagle is deeply rooted in our nation's heritage, folklore, and environment, and has special meaning to many Americans. Eagle images and references are woven into the very fabric of our society, including architecture, music, literature, art, clothing, and commercial products.

G. The Eagle's Comeback and Today's Challenges

We almost lost America's precious eagles due to the effects of the chemical pesticide DDT, destruction of habitat, poaching, and environmental carelessness. By the early 1960s, the count of nesting bald eagles plummeted to about 417 in the lower forty-eight states.

The removal of the bald eagle from the "threatened and endangered" species list was announced by Secretary of the Interior Dirk Kempthorne on June 28, 2007, with the bald eagle Challenger by his side.

The bald eagle is now a protected species. The banning of DDT, strict protection laws, the work of conservationists and environmentalists, and the efforts of organizations like the American Eagle Foundation have all contributed to the bald eagle recovery. These birds have made an amazing comeback: the US Fish & Wildlife Service reports an estimated 143,000 individuals today!

We have made encouraging progress but must continue this commitment until the bald eagle has made a full and healthy recovery. The bald eagle still faces daunting post-delisting challenges—from loss of crucial nesting and foraging habitat, to the threat of contaminants, viruses, and diseases.

Even newer challenges have arisen for our national symbol: guns, traps, wind turbines, power lines, lead ammunition, dangerous chemicals, and general ignorance all pose a constant threat to the bald eagle's future. Read more about the plight of the bald eagle by visiting www.eagles.org.

Glossary

ADULT. A sexually mature eagle, usually four to five years of age or more, identified by white head and tail feathers

BRANCHING. A stage of development when eaglets hop from the nest onto the nest tree's branches before their first flight

BREED. To mate and reproduce

BREEDING SEASON. The period during which a mated eagle pair prepares their nest, mates, lays eggs, and raises offspring (also referred to as nesting season)

BREEDING TERRITORY. The land area defended by a mated eagle pair in which they nest, mate, and reproduce

BROOD. The offspring from a single clutch of eggs

BROOD/BROODING. The act performed by a parent eagle when using its body to warm, shade, or otherwise protect hatched offspring

BROOD PATCH. The area of featherless skin near a parent eagle's abdomen used to incubate eggs or keep hatched eaglets warm

CANOPY. The upper layer of a mature group of trees

CARRION. A decayed or dead animal used as food

CHICK. A young, flightless eaglet

CLUTCH. A single set or group of eggs laid by a female eagle during nesting season

CROP. An area between the neck and stomach where food is stored after consumption and bones of fish and animals are broken down

DOWN. The soft, fuzzy plumage on chicks

EAGLET. A young eagle

EGG CUP. The soft cup formed inside the nest by parent eagles where eggs are laid and incubated

EGG TOOTH. The hard, hooked point near the tip of an eaglet's beak used during hatching to crack out of its shell

FIRST FLIGHT. An eaglet's first attempt to fly away from the nest

FLEDGE/FLEDGLING. An eaglet takes first flight and returns to its nest

FLIGHT FEATHERS. The wing and tail feathers that enable an eagle to sustain flight

FOOD-BEGGING. Communicating through calls for food

FORAGE. To search for and obtain food

GLIDE. To fly in a smooth, even manner with outstretched wings and little apparent movement

HABITAT. An eagle's natural living environment

HATCHING. A process during which an eaglet cracks through and becomes free from its egg shell

HATCHLING. A recently hatched eaglet

HOP-FLAPS. A series of movements when an eaglet hops across the nest while wing-flapping prior to fledging

INCUBATE. To apply body heat while sitting on a clutch of eggs

JUVENILE. A young eagle, under one year old, that is experienced with flight and living away from the nest

MANTLE. An attempt to hide a meal by hunching the shoulders and spreading the wings and/or tail over the food

NARES. Nostrils on the upper portion of an eagle's beak

NEST. A structure consisting of sticks and soft lining prepared by a mated eagle pair for laying eggs and raising offspring

NEST CUP. The soft cup formed inside the nest by parent eagles where eggs are laid and incubated

NESTING SEASON. The period during which a mated eagle pair prepares their nest, mates, lays eggs, and raises offspring

NESTLING. An eaglet incapable of flight and confined to its nest; not yet able to fly

NESTORATIONS. The parent eagles' actions taken to repair or restore the nest

OFFSPRING. The young eaglet(s) produced by a mated eagle pair

PEEPING. The short, penetrating vocalizations of an eagle chick

PERCH. To rest, sit, forage, or stand watch from a tree limb

PIPPING. Process undertaken by an unborn eaglet to crack its eggshell and create a small hole from the inside to break free

PLUMAGE. An eagle's exterior body and flight feathers

PREDATOR. An animal that forages other animals for food to survive

PREEN. To groom, position, or straighten feathers with the beak

PREY. An animal foraged for food

RAPTOR. A large bird having talons and a sharp, hooked beak and a carnivorous diet that hunts and captures live prey or carrion for food

ROOST. To sleep, rest, or find shelter at night, during the day, or during inclement weather

SNAG. A dead tree

SOAR. To mount the air with an ascending, circular flight using little wing motion

TALON. Long, sharp, curved claw on the end of an eagle's foot

TARSUS/TARSI. The ankle area of an eagle's leg and foot

TERRITORY. The area defended by a mated eagle pair in which they nest, mate, and reproduce

WINGER-CIZE. An eaglet's flapping movement to exercise its wings

Other Schiffer Books
by Gorrow and Koppie

Just Released

Inside an Osprey's Nest
A Photographic Journey through Nesting Season
ISBN 978-0-7643-5200-3
Two fostered osprey chicks get a new mom and dad in this heartwarming, true account featuring the Chesapeake Conservancy Osprey Nest Cam family.

Inside a Bald Eagle's Nest
A Photographic Journey through the American Bald Eagle Nesting Season
ISBN 978-0-7643-4464-0
Travel with a mated pair of American bald eagles as they raise a family of chicks just outside of Washington, DC.

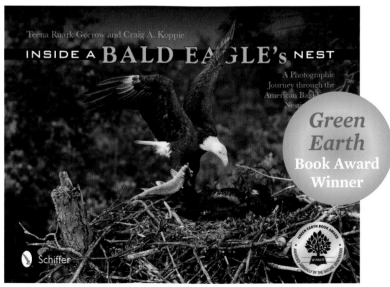